I0820963

DINOSAURS

ARCHAEOPTERYX

BY ANGELA LIM

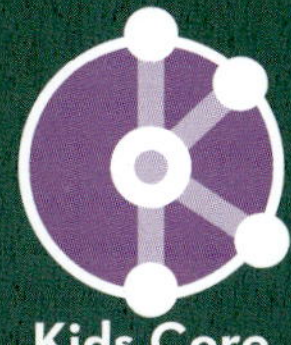

Kids Core
An Imprint of Abdo Publishing
abdobooks.com

abdobooks.com

Printed in the United States of America, North Mankato, Minnesota.
052025
092025

THIS BOOK CONTAINS RECYCLED MATERIALS

Cover Photo: Shutterstock Images
Interior Photos: Corey Ford/iStockphoto, 4–5; iStockphoto, 6, 17 (bottom); Shutterstock Images, 9, 17 (top), 23, 28–29; Esther van Hulsen/Stocktrek Images/Science Source, 10; Daniel Eskridge/Shutterstock Images, 12–13, 15; Michael Long/Science Source, 16; Grafissimo/DigitalVision Vectors/Getty Images, 18; Chris Hellier/Science Source, 20–21; duncan1890/DigitalVision Vectors/Getty Images, 24; Moviestore Collection Ltd./Alamy, 26

Editor: Kari Cornell
Series Design: Mary Shaw

Library of Congress Control Number: 2024949186

Publisher's Cataloging-in-Publication Data

Names: Lim, Angela, author.
Title: Archaeopteryx / by Angela Lim
Description: Minneapolis, Minnesota: Abdo Publishing, 2026 | Series: Dinosaurs | Includes online resources and index.
Identifiers: ISBN 9781098297336 (lib. bdg.) | ISBN 9798384919858 (ebook)
Subjects: LCSH: Archaeopteryx--Juvenile literature. | Dinosaurs--Juvenile literature. | Carnivorous animals--Juvenile literature. | Paleontology--Juvenile literature. | Extinct animals--Juvenile literature.
Classification: DDC 568.19--dc23

CONTENTS

Scientists believe *Archaeopteryx* was able to glide and flap its wings to fly short distances when needed.

A SOARING DINOSAUR

An *Archaeopteryx* (ahr-kee-AHP-ter-ihks) perches in a tree. The sun shines on its feathered wings. Its long tail hangs down.

The small dinosaur scans the waters of a lagoon. Dragonflies flit over the surface. A small reptile emerges from the water.

The feathers at the tips of *Archaeopteryx*'s wings were black. Black feathers are sturdier for flight.

It crawls onto dry land. The *Archaeopteryx* takes off. It glides toward the reptile. The dinosaur pins its **prey** to the ground with its claws. It tears into its meal with sharp teeth.

Staying on the ground is dangerous for the small dinosaur. Larger **predators** may attack it. The *Archaeopteryx* flaps its wings as soon as it finishes eating its meal. It flies into the trees where it's safe.

What Are Dinosaurs?

Dinosaurs are reptiles. They lived on Earth about 250 million years ago during the Mesozoic Era. This era is divided into three periods. They are the Triassic, Jurassic, and Cretaceous Periods. *Archaeopteryx* lived during the late Jurassic. It lived about 149 to 145 million years ago.

Paleontologists study fossils to learn about animal and plant life from a long time ago.

Fossils are the remains of animals and plants. They include bones, teeth, and feathers. After an animal dies, these body parts are buried underground. Over time, they become rock.

Archaeopteryx fossils were a major discovery. The fossils show sharp teeth and a strong tail. Other dinosaurs have these

What Is Evolution?

Evolution describes how life today came to exist. Living things **adapt** to their surroundings over time. Certain features and behaviors helped them survive. These characteristics are passed down to their young. For example, flight helped *Archaeopteryx* survive. This ability was passed down over millions of years. Birds would eventually **evolve** from *Archaeopteryx* and other birdlike dinosaurs.

Unlike some other feathered dinosaurs, *Archaeopteryx* had feathers that were meant for flight, similar to modern birds.

characteristics. But the fossils also have wings with feathers. *Archaeopteryx*'s wings looked like the wings of a bird. Scientists believe the dinosaur was an **ancestor** to modern birds.

Archaeopteryx had a bony tail that was likely used for balance, flight, and display.

Learning about *Archaeopteryx* has helped scientists understand more about evolution and life on Earth today.

PRIMARY SOURCE

Field Museum president Julian Siggers talked about the importance of discovering the *Archaeopteryx* fossil:

> The top-level message is that dinosaurs didn't go **extinct**, they actually evolved into birds.

Source: Patty Wetli. "The Field Museum Now Has an Incredibly Rare Fossil Proving Birds Are Dinosaurs." *WTTW News*, 6 May 2024, news.wttw.com. Accessed 28 Sept. 2024.

Comparing Texts

Think about the quote. Does it support the information in this chapter? Or does it give a new perspective? Explain how in two or three sentences.

Archaeopteryx likely hunted insects and small animals while perched on tree branches.

ARCHAEOPTERYX FEATURES

Paleontologists know the size of *Archaeopteryx* based on its skeleton. The smallest individuals were about the size of a blue jay. The biggest were similar in size to a large chicken. *Archaeopteryx* weighed about 2 pounds (0.9 kg).

Archaeopteryx shared similarities with land dinosaurs. It had a long, bony tail. For many dinosaurs, a long tail helped with balance. *Archaeopteryx* likely used its tail to balance as well.

Fossils show that *Archaeopteryx* had teeth. This is also similar to most dinosaurs. This dinosaur's teeth were sharp and cone shaped.

Feather Color

It is rare for paleontologists to know the color of a dinosaur. Colors are not usually part of fossils. But sometimes tiny body parts that produce color are fossilized. Scientists found these body parts in an *Archaeopteryx* feather. They believe *Archaeopteryx*'s wings were black. But the feathers may have been a lighter color with black tips.

Archaeopteryx had claws in the middle of its wings. It likely used the claws to catch prey and grab tree branches.

Like other dinosaurs, *Archaeopteryx* had claws. It was able to move each claw independently. *Archaeopteryx* had three claws on each leg. Modern birds also have three fingers. But they are inside the wings.

For its body size, *Archaeopteryx* had a very long, bony tail.

The bones are fused together. They cannot be moved separately.

Archaeopteryx shared other characteristics with modern birds. Like birds, it had feathered wings and a similar skeleton. *Archaeopteryx* also had thin, hollow bones. It had a wishbone. This was a V-shaped bone in its breast. There were only a few other dinosaurs that had this bone. They included *Tyrannosaurus rex* and *Velociraptor*.

Modern Birds vs. *Archaeopteryx*

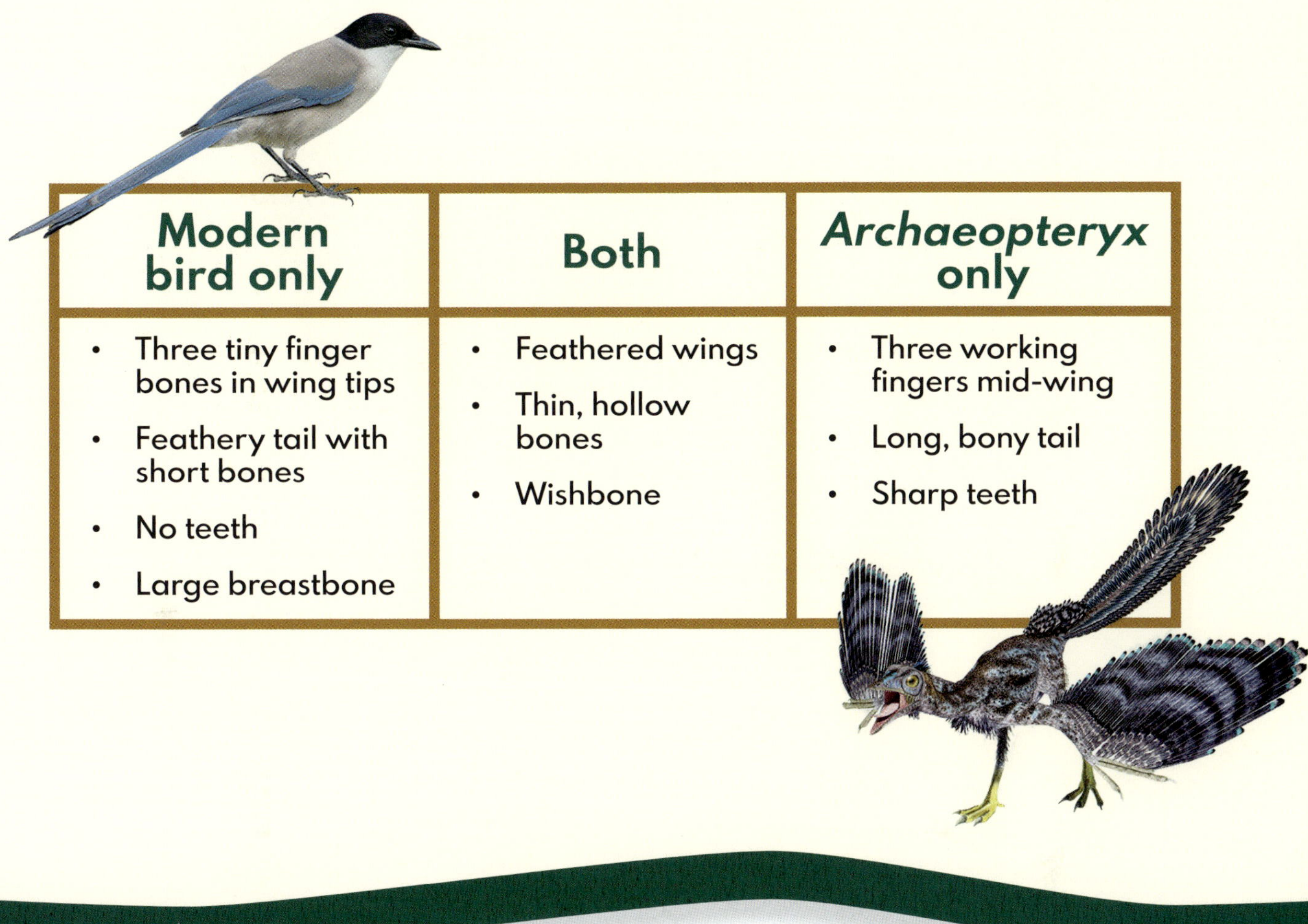

Modern bird only	Both	*Archaeopteryx* only
• Three tiny finger bones in wing tips • Feathery tail with short bones • No teeth • Large breastbone	• Feathered wings • Thin, hollow bones • Wishbone	• Three working fingers mid-wing • Long, bony tail • Sharp teeth

Archaeopteryx had many similarities to modern birds. But it also had features in common with other dinosaurs.

Archaeopteryx Behavior

Scientists are still learning about *Archaeopteryx*.

The dinosaur had wings similar to modern birds.

Early illustrations of *Archaeopteryx* include rows of teeth. Some modern birds have spikes in their mouths, but these are not teeth. Modern birds do not have teeth.

It was likely able to fly only short distances. But some scientists think it could not fly. They think it could only glide, like a flying squirrel.

Paleontologists have discovered *Archaeopteryx* fossils in present-day Germany. During the late Jurassic, this area was a tropical lagoon. *Archaeopteryx* lived on land. It preyed upon small animals in the area. The dinosaur's sharp teeth show that it was a **carnivore**. But the exact diet of *Archaeopteryx* is unknown. It might have eaten insects, small reptiles, or small mammals.

Explore Online

Visit the website below. Does it give new details about *Archaeopteryx* that weren't in Chapter Two?

Archaeopteryx

abdocorelibrary.com/archaeopteryx

Fossils of *Archaeopteryx* show imprints of wings with feathers.

KEY ARCHAEOPTERYX FINDINGS

Hermann von Meyer was a German paleontologist. In 1861, he described an *Archaeopteryx* fossil. He was the first person to do so. The fossil was a single feather. It was the oldest-known fossilized feather at the time.

He discovered it in southern Germany. Nearly all *Archaeopteryx* fossils were later found in this region.

The name *Archaeopteryx* means "ancient wing." The fossil was almost 150 million years old. There were no birds back then. Scientists wondered where the feather had come from. The discovery of the *Archaeopteryx* feather took place during an important turning point in scientific history.

Charles Darwin had published his book *On the Origin of Species* in 1859. In this book, Darwin explained the theory of evolution. He said that animals **adapted** over time in order to survive. Paleontologists thought that the feather supported Darwin's idea.

Compared to other dinosaur skeletons that take up entire rooms in museums, *Archaeopteryx* skeletons are small enough to fit on a table.

In 1868, biologist Thomas Huxley wrote a paper. He described *Archaeopteryx* as a link between dinosaurs and birds. But it took many years for scientists to agree. Some thought birds and dinosaurs were not linked by evolution.

British biologist Thomas Huxley became known as "Darwin's bulldog" for his strong support of Charles Darwin's theory of evolution.

This changed in 1996. Other feathered dinosaurs were discovered. The fossils showed many similarities with modern birds.

Most scientists today describe *Archaeopteryx* as a birdlike dinosaur. Chicago's Field Museum displays an *Archaeopteryx* fossil. Another one is on display in Thermopolis, Wyoming.

In Pop Culture

Archaeopteryx is shown in pop culture. It was briefly shown in the 1940 Disney movie *Fantasia*.

The Earliest Bird

Birds evolved from dinosaurs. But it is difficult to determine exactly when this happened. The earliest known bird fossil dates from about 66.7 million years ago. The fossil belonged to a prehistoric bird called the wonderchicken.

A pink *Archaeopteryx*, a *Triceratops*, *pictured*, and other dinosaurs appeared in the "Rite of Spring" portion of the movie *Fantasia*.

It takes off from a tree to escape a predator. *Archaeopteryx* probably flew in real life. But it likely could not fly far.

The feathered dinosaur was also in *Ice Age: Dawn of the Dinosaurs* (2009). The movie shows mammoths and dinosaurs living together. But this is not historically accurate. Dinosaurs went **extinct** 63 million years before the Ice Age (2.6 million–11,000 years ago).

Archaeopteryx may not appear in many movies. But it plays a huge role in science. It shows how birds **evolved** from dinosaurs. It is an important evolutionary link. By studying *Archaeopteryx*, scientists discover connections between life in the past and life today.

Further Evidence

Look at the website below. Does it give any new evidence to support Chapter Three?

Archaeopteryx

abdocorelibrary.com/archaeopteryx

DINO DETAILS

Three claws at mid-wing that could move independently
Cone-shaped teeth for eating other animals

Glossary

adapt
to change in order to survive in a habitat over a long period of time

ancestor
an early animal from which other animals evolved

carnivore
an animal that eats primarily meat

evolve
to change over time

extinct
no longer exists

paleontologist
a scientist who studies fossils

predator
an animal that hunts other animals

prey
an animal that is food for a predator

Online Resources

To learn more about *Archaeopteryx* and late-Jurassic dinosaurs, visit our free resource websites below.

Visit **abdocorelibrary.com** or scan this QR code for free Common Core resources for teachers and students, including vetted activities, multimedia, and booklinks, for deeper subject comprehension.

Visit **abdobooklinks.com** or scan this QR code for free additional online weblinks for further learning. These links are routinely monitored and updated to provide the most current information available.

Learn More

Dinosaur Atlas. National Geographic, 2022.

Golkar, Golriz. *Velociraptor.* Abdo, 2026.

Woodward, John. *The Dinosaur Book.* DK, 2023.

Index

About the Author

Angela Lim is an MFA student in poetry at Indiana University. *Stegosaurus* is her favorite dinosaur.